W9-BRS-526

ideals HOMETOWN

The gentle twilight wraps a soft blue shawl
About the shoulders of the drowsy day
And pins it with a single star. The call
Of mothers brings the children in from play
To prayers, and bed. Beyond the mountain's rim
The blacksmith, night, is forging a new moon
Into a shining cutlass; and the hymn
The katydids and crickets softly croon
Hangs in the quiet air.
God must look down, and smile,
Upon the peace of this small town.

Jessie Wilmore Murton

ISBN 0-8249-1027-3 350

Publisher, Patricia A. Pingry
Editor/Ideals, Kathleen S. Pohl
Managing Editor, Marybeth Owens
Production Manager, Mark Brunner
Photographic Editor, Gerald Koser
Manuscript Editor, Naomi Galbreath
Research Editor, Linda Robinson

IDEALS—Vol. 41, No. 4 April MCMLXXXIV IDEALS (ISSN 0019-137X) is published eight times a year,
February, March, April, June, August, September, November, December
by IDEALS PUBLISHING CORPORATION, 11315 Watertown Plank Road, Milwaukee, Wis. 53226
Second class postage paid at Milwaukee, Wisconsin and additional mailing offices.
Copyright © MCMLXXXIV by IDEALS PUBLISHING CORPORATION.
POSTMASTER: Send address changes to Ideals, Post Office Box 2100, Milwaukee, Wis. 53201
All rights reserved. Title IDEALS registered U.S. Patent Office.
Published simultaneously in Canada.

ONE YEAR SUBSCRIPTION—eight consecutive issues as published—$15.95
TWO YEAR SUBSCRIPTION—sixteen consecutive issues as published—$27.95
SINGLE ISSUE—$3.50
Outside U.S.A., add $4.00 per subscription year for postage and handling

Front and back covers
HARRISVILLE, NEW HAMPSHIRE
Fred Dole

The Home Town
by Edgar A. Guest

It doesn't matter much be its buildings great or
   small,
The home town, the home town, is the best town,
   after all.
The cities of the millions have the sun and stars
   above,
But they lack the friendly faces of the few you've
   learned to love,
And with all their pomp of riches and with all their
   teeming throngs,
The heart of man is rooted in the town where he
   belongs.

There are places good to visit, there are cities fair
   to see,
There are haunts of charm and beauty where at
   times it's good to be,
But the humblest little hamlet sings a melody to
   some,
And no matter where they travel it is calling them
   to come;
Though cities rise to greatness and are gay with
   gaudy dress,
There is something in the home town which no other
   towns possess.

The home town has a treasure which the distance
   cannot gain,
It is there the hearts are kindest, there the gentlest
   friends remain;
It is there a mystic something seems to permeate
   the air
To set the weary wanderer to wishing he were
   there;
And be it great or humble, it still holds mankind
   in thrall,
For the home town, the home town, is the best town
   after all.

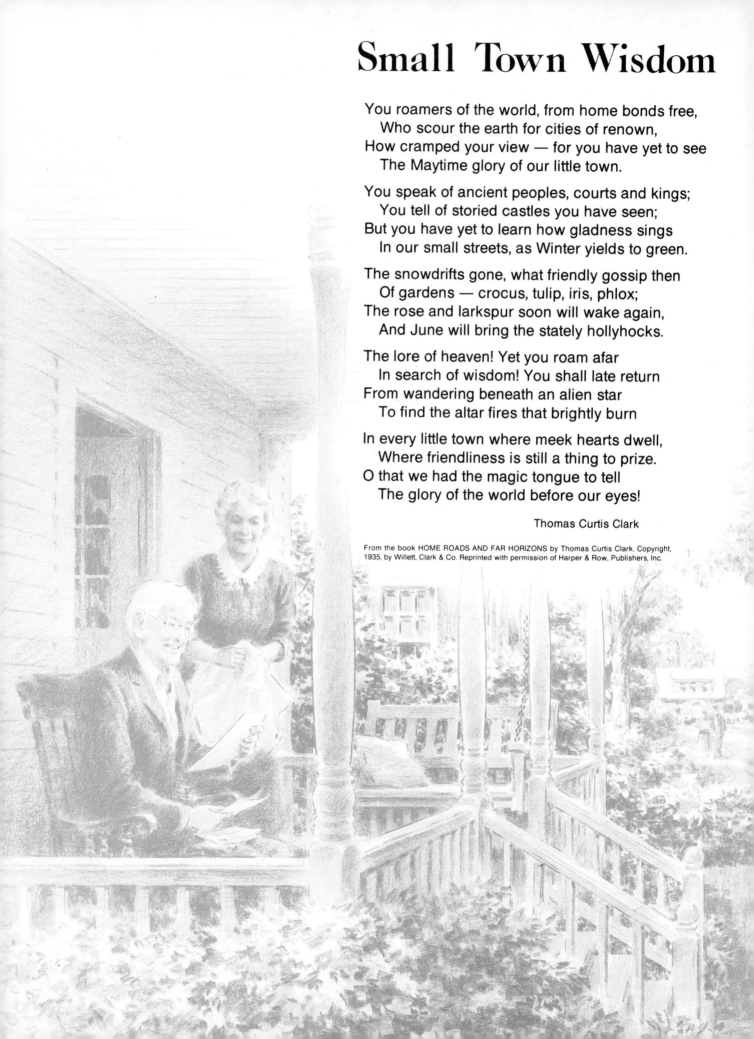

Small Town Wisdom

You roamers of the world, from home bonds free,
　Who scour the earth for cities of renown,
How cramped your view — for you have yet to see
　The Maytime glory of our little town.

You speak of ancient peoples, courts and kings;
　You tell of storied castles you have seen;
But you have yet to learn how gladness sings
　In our small streets, as Winter yields to green.

The snowdrifts gone, what friendly gossip then
　Of gardens — crocus, tulip, iris, phlox;
The rose and larkspur soon will wake again,
　And June will bring the stately hollyhocks.

The lore of heaven! Yet you roam afar
　In search of wisdom! You shall late return
From wandering beneath an alien star
　To find the altar fires that brightly burn

In every little town where meek hearts dwell,
　Where friendliness is still a thing to prize.
O that we had the magic tongue to tell
　The glory of the world before our eyes!

Thomas Curtis Clark

From the book HOME ROADS AND FAR HORIZONS by Thomas Curtis Clark. Copyright, 1935, by Willett, Clark & Co. Reprinted with permission of Harper & Row, Publishers, Inc.

I Remember a Town

I remember a town and a pleasant street
   Where the maple trees flung high
Their shading branches through summer days
   Beneath a calm blue sky.

I remember the children who ran and played
   On corners beneath the lights;
Their shrill young voices gay and sweet,
   Those quiet starlit nights.

I shall always remember the popcorn man
   And the concerts in the square;
Kindly faces of those I loved;
   Almost I see them there.

I remember a man with warm brown eyes
   In a little grocery store,
Who for my penny always gave
   Six chocolates, sometimes more.

I remember a town though the years are long
   And miles lie in between;
A town that is dearest to my heart
   Of all the towns I've seen.

Sheila Stinson

The American Small Town

I have just returned from another of my periods of wandering over America visiting many states, talking to farmers out on the wide plains of Texas and little Southern cotton-patch farmers, going to many cities, going in and out of many, many towns. Now here I am back in my own town and happy.

Familiar walks to be taken, roads to be driven over in the car, familiar faces to be seen on the street! Places to be visited, certain country roads that lead up into the hills, spots by the river bank . . . .

The shapes of the hills about our town, the little bunches of trees on certain hills . . . . I am a confirmed small-towner, and you know how all we small-towners feel about our town, our pride in it, our belief that it is the best town on earth, our hopes for its future. With me it's a case of love. You can see the beauty of many women and yet love only one. Perhaps I am in love with my own town of Marion and my Virginia country because I have been here for a long time now. I realize the same thing might have happened to me in Kansas, in Georgia, or Connecticut. Love of a town and a countryside, like love of a woman, may be a matter of proximity. Whatever the reason, my town and countryside seem especially beautiful to me.

Perhaps only a passionate traveler like myself can realize how lucky he is to be able to call a small town his home. My work is constantly calling me away from Marion, but I always hunger to get back. There is in the life of the small town a possibility of intimacy, a chance to know others — an intimacy oftentimes frightening, but which can be healing. Day after day, under all sorts of circumstances, in sickness and health, in good fortune and bad, we small-towners are close to one another and know each other in ways the city man can never experience. A man goes away and comes back. Certain people have died. Babies have been born. Children of yesterday have suddenly become young men and women. Life has been going on. Still nothing has really changed. On the streets, day after day, mostly the same faces. There is this narrow but fascinating panorama. In a way it is too intimate. Life can never be intimate enough.

Sherwood Anderson

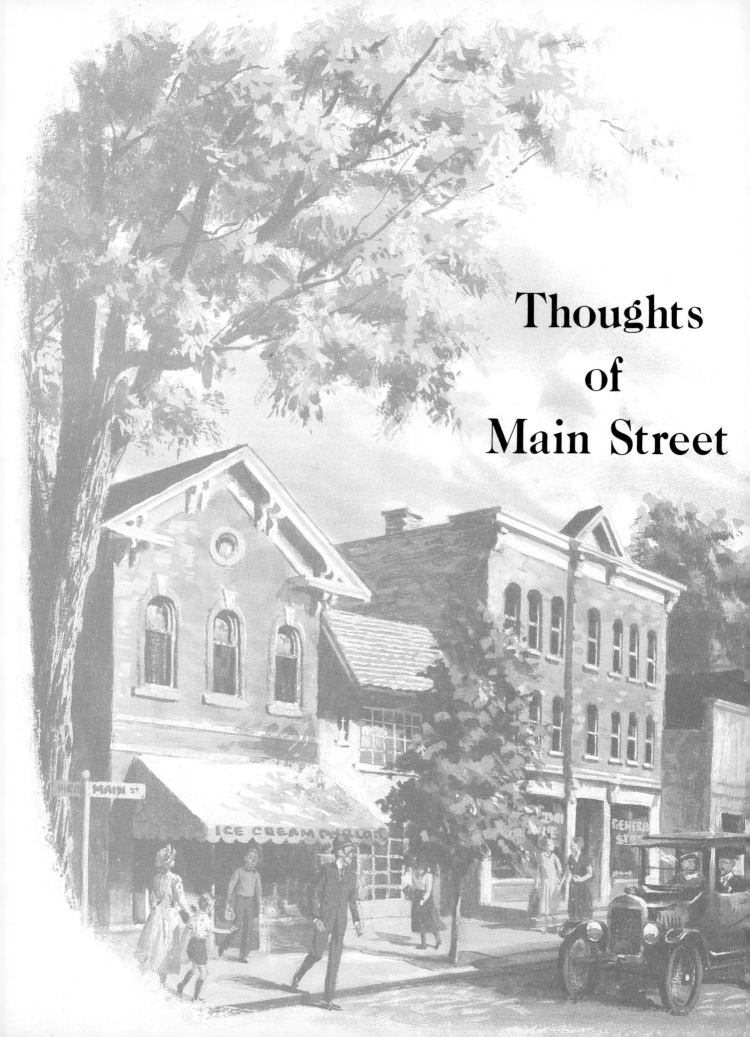

Thoughts
of
Main Street

My mind is filled with sheerest joy
When in my thoughts I go
To wander down the small Main Street
I loved those years ago.

Now once again the barber nods
Beneath his visored cap,
While by his pole...red, white, and blue...
An old dog takes a nap.

The general store comes into view,
And anxiously I stand
Before the kegs of candy
With a penny in my hand.

The druggist bids me come inside
To see his fine array
Of perfumes, health and grooming aids,
And jewelry sparkling gay.

The popcorn stand still fills the air
With buttery delight;
The ice-cream social in the park
Is part of Wednesday night.

Two laughing boys race merrily,
Their faces full of cheer.
Their marble games, their nature hikes,
Come back through all the years.

What fun to see each smiling face,
To hear each fond hello,
To walk the Main Street once again
I came to love and know.

Craig E. Sathoff

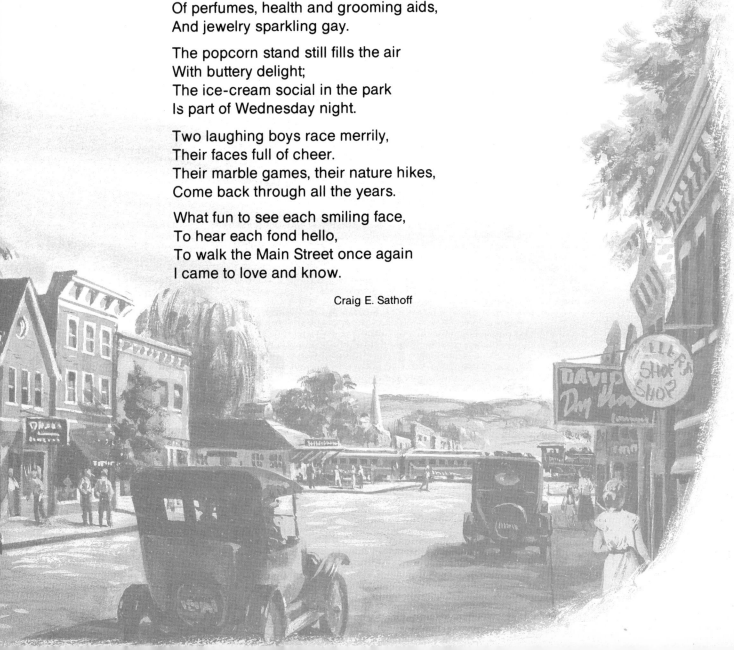

Those Old Model T's

Those old Model T's, those Model T Fords,
Had no stereo but two running boards.
Side curtains and all, they were strictly first class,
With dirt stains on windows of cracked isinglass.

The gas tank was large: twelve gallons it held.
It was cunningly placed so that you were compelled
To hop out of your car (a neat little trick)
And measure the gas with a gasoline stick.

The checking of oil required, if you please,
Lying down on the ground (with what grace! with what ease!)
And reaching beneath to discover the pair
Of valves that were hidden conveniently there.

The high-pressure tires, in the peak of good style,
With fifty-pound pressure ran four thousand miles.
Size thirty by three with a clincher-rim grip,
A flat tire was sure on a fifty-mile trip.

There's no radio here, giving forth with the news;
No broadcaster here, expounding his views.
Power brakes, power steering were not to be had
And there were no gimmicks that just might go bad.

These cars, with high bodies and doors that were small,
Meant easier entry for folks fat or tall.
But there were no doors where the drivers would ride,
So they would climb up and hop over the side.

Sometime if I may, just for old time's sake,
I would drive one more time in a car of this make.
Daredevil I'd be, with a daredevil smile,
And I'd push her way up to near forty mile.

Dana Craig

Photo opposite
MODEL T FORD COUPE
Fred Sieb

Harmony Heritage

No one can say for sure when or where the first barbershop chords were sung, but one may safely suggest they were heard many years after the seige of Troy.

The expressions "barbershop music" and "barbershop harmony" very possibly survive from an English custom now obsolete in the land of its origin. There, during the sixteenth, seventeenth, and early eighteenth centuries, the barbershop was "a regular haunt for music."

Samuel Pepys, the noted diarist, tells us that John Milton once wrote a few lines of comment on the musical aspect of barbershops, saying that a lute or cittern, both forerunners of the modern guitar, hung on the wall for use by waiting customers. Barbers became proficient in the rendering of melodies during those moments when they were not engaged with customers. Music-making was a pleasant way to pass the time, and many barbers "came to possess some repute as performers."

In speculating on the origins of barbershop music, one might imagine barbershops as places where men might "let down their hair." In the course of a discussion of weather, politics, sports, and women, the barbershop's clientele could quite naturally join together in song.

English barbershops continued to be exclusively tonsorial parlors into the early eighteenth century. But barbers set aside their stringed instruments and lost their enthusiasm for music when new money-making and time-consuming activities were introduced into their trade. Blood-letting, tooth-pulling, and particularly periwig-making soon supplanted the long-standing musical pastime.

As English barbers abandoned their musical activities, never to pursue them again, the popular concept of the barbershop as a music salon also disappeared.

Barbers in America, like their ancestral cousins in the Old World, took up the playing of stringed instruments. Many became masters on the guitar, and this eventually reflected on all barbers. Steinert, a respected Boston piano manufacturer, once spoke the following of a man with whom he lodged in Georgia, in about 1860: "As once upon a time he had been a barber, he knew how to play the guitar."

The first American "barbers' music" was probably strummed and sung in the South, for our Puritan forefathers would hardly have tolerated such frivolity. The South, with its light-hearted, socially-oriented society, presented ideal conditions for planting seeds of harmony that were destined to sprout all over the continent. In Williamsburg, Virginia, the Raleigh Tavern pictures of resident colonial gentlemen discussing the day's affairs while gathered around the hearth, seated at the tables, and standing at the bar reflect leisurely customs of Mother England. The making of barbershop music may well have held a secure place in the colony which prided itself in maintaining an English way of life.

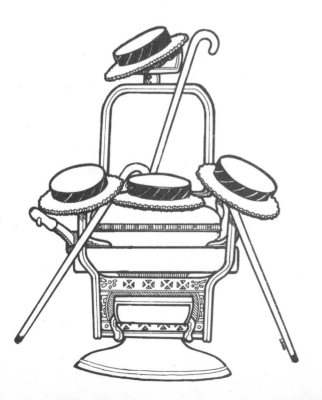

The Corner Grocery

by Patricia Heydenberk

The corner grocery was a family affair with no budget for advertising, no neon signs and, often, no corner. A simple wooden board with the family name made do. Willis's and Olson's were noted for their meat; Curtis's for fresh vegetables; Campbell's for low-priced canned goods; and Harold's — across from the elementary school — for the best penny candies.

Inside, the warmth of wooden floors, shelves, counters, and vegetable crates welcomed young and old. And so did the storekeepers, greeting each customer by name.

Only two or three brands stocked the shelves. Fresh fruits and vegetables were mostly bought in season, with strawberries for shortcake in May, the first watermelon for the Fourth of July, and corn-on-the-cob for weeks after. A white-aproned butcher stood ready to cut beef to order, grind hamburger, or wrap a chosen chicken.

Contrary to modern marketing strategy, items were grouped conveniently. Meat, produce, and milk occupied one area. Baked, canned, boxed, and household products had their own special sections. This arrangement was permanent, and most any kid could find what was needed if he could remember what he came for or if he could read the shopping list. Of course, if he couldn't read it, the grocer's wife, Bessie, would do it for him.

Mothers would complain if sugar went up a penny-a-pound, but their loyalty to the neighborhood corner grocery remained strong. For when times were tight, cash wasn't needed. Family credit "slips" were kept in the cash drawer to be paid on paydays. With a note from Mother, even a child was allowed to sign the back of a slip. This way, children became aware of family finances.

If this accounting method seems unsophisticated, the transaction involving the return of soda pop bottles was not. The bottles, at two cents for regular and five cents for the big ones, were collected by kids and exchanged for penny candy. Jawbreakers, licorice sticks, Double Bubble gum, Hershey's bars, Baby Ruths, Butterfingers, and Three Musketeers ranged from two for a penny to a nickel apiece. Two Pepsi, one Squirt, and one big Coke bottle presented a multitude of possibilities to the indecisive kids and required infinite patience on the part of Bessie.

Photo opposite
COUNTRY STORE INTERIOR
Harold M. Lambert Studios, Inc.

Far out beyond the city's lights, away from din and roar,
The cricket chirps of summer nights beneath the country store;
The drygoods boxes ricked about afford a welcome seat
For weary tillers of the ground, who here on evenings meet.

A swinging sign of ancient make, and one above the door,
Proclaim that William Henry Blake is owner of the store;
Here everything from jam to tweed, from silks to ginghams bright,
Is spread before the folk who need from early morn till night.

Tea, sugar, coffee (browned or green), molasses, grindstones, tar,
Suspenders, peanuts, navy beans, and homemade vinegar,
Fine combs, wash ringers, rakes, false hair, paints, rice, and looking
    glasses,
Side saddles, hominy, crockery ware, and seeds for garden grasses.
Lawn mowers, candies, books to read, corn planter, household goods,
Tobacco, salt, and clover seed, horsewhips and knitted hoods,
Canned goods, shoe blacking, lime and nails, straw hats and carpet slippers,
Prunes, buttons, codfish, bridal veils, cranberries, clocks, and clippers.

Umbrellas, candles, scythes and hats, caps, boots and shoes and bacon,
Thread, nutmegs, pins and Rough on Rats, for cash or produce taken;
Birdseed, face powder, matches, files, ink, onions and many more,
Are found in heaps and stacks and piles within the country store.

Author Unknown

What Makes a Puddle?

Phillip always wondered things; he always wondered why
The sky was blue, the grass was green, and how the birds might fly.
His favorite time was Sunday, after lunch with Grampa Joe;
They'd take a walk for exercise and talk an hour or so.

Phil took big steps to match Gramp's steps and listened to him hum.
Together they would whittle sticks while chewing juicy gum.
They'd often find a place to rest, a log or rock or hill,
And ponder things of interest, especially to Phil.

"Questions, questions all the time," Grampa'd always say.
"Just let'em fly...I'm ready...What'cha need to know today?"
"I'm puzzled 'bout the puddles...some are wide and some are small.
Sometimes they're here and then they're gone. What happens to them all?"

"You want to know what makes a puddle?" Grampa said, "No doubt...
It's when it rains...the waters pool...with no place to run out."
Then Phillip asked, "How does the rain know where to stop and rest?"
"It looks for holes and cracks and things, to settle in, I guess."

"I understand," said Phillip, "just why the puddles stay.
But answer for me Grampa...what makes puddles go away?"
"That's why we have the sun, my boy, to warm and dry the ground.
And the wind is mighty helpful as it blows the wet around."

Then Grampa took his big, rough hand and held it out to Phil
And said, "It's time to get along...here take this, if you will."
He handed Phil his pocketwatch...he trusted him, you see...
He said, "My boy, here's somethin' for your curiosity."

The whole next week Phil kept the watch, to think about and question,
Till Sunday, when the walk again was Grampa Joe's suggestion.
"Still got my watch?" asked Grampa Joe, before he carved his sticks.
"Yes sir," said Phillip wondering, "now please tell me why it ticks."

Barbara Brandt

Homemade Ice Cream

Homemade ice cream is never old-fashioned. One of the best treats on any hot summer afternoon is a frosty dish piled high with creamy, homemade ice cream. The summer ritual is dear to most of our childhood memories. It is not hard to recall the hand-cranked ice cream freezer churning and clanking out the cooling treats on hot afternoons or the happy anticipation of licking the cream-laden dasher.

Interestingly, ice cream is not an American invention. It is a romantic world traveler with its precise origin unknown. However, homemade ice cream is an American invention thanks to a New Jersey hostess, Nancy Johnson. In 1846, she devised a crank and paddle, freezer-in-a-bucket machine that allowed the average home-maker to make the dessert with ease. The principle of ice cream making has not changed.

Most modern ice cream freezers are electric powered, but hand-cranked models have been rescued from attics, dusted off, and made to work as well today as they did a generation ago. Purists claim the best homemade ice cream is produced by churning a cream or custard-base mixture in a hand-cranked or electric ice cream freezer, using ice and rock salt.

Strawberry Ice Cream

- 2 eggs
- 1 cup sugar
- 3 cups milk
- 3 cups heavy cream
- ½ teaspoon vanilla
- ⅛ teaspoon salt
- 1 quart crushed strawberries, sweetened to taste

In a large bowl, beat eggs until foamy. Gradually add the sugar, beating until thickened. Add milk, cream, vanilla, and salt. Blend in fruit. Chill. Churn-freeze. Makes about 4 quarts.

Vanilla Ice Cream

- 1½ cups sugar
- ¼ cup flour
- ⅛ teaspoon salt
- 2 cups milk
- 4 eggs, slightly beaten
- 4 cups cream
- 1 tablespoon vanilla

Combine sugar, flour, and salt in a large saucepan; stir in milk. Cook over medium heat, stirring constantly until mixture thickens. Boil 1 minute. Cool slightly. Stir half the warm mixture slowly into beaten eggs in a medium-size bowl. Stir egg mixture back into saucepan. Return to heat and cook over medium heat, not allowing it to boil. Cook 1 minute, stirring constantly. Pour into large bowl. Stir in cream and vanilla. Chill at least 2 hours. Pour mixture into a 4 to 6 quart freezer can; freeze, following directions of your freezer. Makes about 2 quarts.

Chocolate Ice Cream

- 1 quart milk
- 1 cup cocoa
- 1 cup light corn syrup
- 5 eggs
- 2 cups sugar
- 1 quart heavy cream
- 1 tablespoon vanilla

In 2-quart saucepan, combine 2 cups of the milk, cocoa, and corn syrup. Bring to a boil over medium heat, stirring constantly. Cool. In a large mixing bowl, beat eggs until foamy; gradually beat in sugar. Add cocoa mixture. Stir in remaining 2 cups milk, cream, and vanilla. Chill. Churn-freeze. Makes about 1 gallon.

Photo opposite
ICE CREAM DELIGHTS
Gerald Koser

School Is Out

You can hear the merry whistle
And the laughter loud and clear;
There's happiness unequaled
At this special time of year.
There's a girl's delighted giggle
And a boy's impatient shout,
And you know without a question
It is summer — school is out!

You can feel the warmth of summer
And the sun against your cheek,
Smell the fragrance of roses,
Hear the babbling of the creek.
Kids are barefoot in the country,
Hiking over hill and glen.
Life is carefree, days are happy,
Telling school is out again!

There is lots of time for dreaming,
Picnics in the shaded wood,
Camping out along the river
Where the fishing's really good.
What a thrill to go in swimming!
These are joys without a doubt.
All the kids are in their glory,
'Cause it's summer. School is out!

Garnett Ann Schultz

Wild Trail

The road that led to the country school
Was a small dirt road and long,
But a short-cut ran through the fields and woods,
Where I strolled with a lilting song.

Oh, many a day I walked alone,
So far as the world could see...
But a stranger crew you never met
Than the ones who walked with me.

Sometimes old Daniel Boone himself
Blazed the trail through the towering trees,
And often Hiawatha would lead the way,
Then vanish upon the breeze.

And then sometimes it was Robin Hood,
Or a knight with a blue steel lance,
And once I met Ponce de Leon...
Oh, life was full of romance!

A concrete highway now leads to school,
I have paused there, but in vain.
I looked for the trail that led through the woods...
I never could find it again.

Mary E. Linton

The Candy Store

A licorice whip or jelly bean
Transports me to a bygone scene,
Where once I stood with hungry eyes,
And murmured little yearning sighs
For gingerbread and lemon drops
And chicken corn and lollipops.

For there I'd stand in mute despair,
An indecisive millionaire,
With fifty ways I might disburse
The two whole pennies in my purse.

So teetering from toe to heel,
I'd wheedle me a special "deal"
For one of *those* and two of *this*,
A jujube and a taffy kiss,
A sour ball, a slice of gum,
A hoarhound drop, a sugar plum.

The flight of memory takes me back
To the penny candy in the striped
   paper sack.

Phyllis I. Rosenteur

Painting opposite
CANDY STORE
John Slobodnik

The Ragman

"Rags, I say! Any rags today?"
   It was such a welcome sound.
The hooves clapped a beat
On the city street
   As the ragman drove around.

Soon the windows rattled open,
   Attic doors swung wide,
Then dozens of bags
Of old clothes and rags
   Appeared at the wagon's side.

"Rags, I say! Any rags today?"
   He sang as he moved along.
And the neighbors smiled,
For a little while,
   To hear the ragman's song.

The Vegetable Man

In horse and wagon days gone by,
   When the vegetable man drove 'round,
Fresh roasting ears
Or asparagus spears
   Showed up all over town.

Sometimes he brought green onions
   Or berries, red and sweet.
He'd weigh them all
And then he'd call
   His wares on every street.

"I have cherries! Fresh red cherries!"
   No shop along the mall
Can e'er replace
That friendly face
   Or sound the vendor's call.

The Scissors Grinder

Remember the scissors grinder?
　His bell had a special sound,
Like "a-RING-tee-tum!"
It would really hum
　As he pushed his cart around.

His honing wheel and whetstone
　Made knives and scissors gleam.
Each sickle and blade
Were renewed by his trade
　And his mowers cut like a dream!

Remember the wheel and its turning,
　Removing the rust that was rife?
What tales he would tell
And his grinder as well:
　He brightened the pathways of life.

Street Photographer

On certain sunny afternoons
　Where children loved to play,
There'd come the beat
Of a pony's feet
　Along the cobbled way.

The smiling street photographer,
　With his camera and his hood,
Sold pony rides
And prints besides
　In each friendly neighborhood.

Unlike some passing fancies,
　Replaced by fashion's rage —
His pony's gone,
His work lives on
　In each family album page.

Poetry by Alice Leedy Mason

Old Houses

I love old houses! There is dignity
Of years upon each timber and each stone;
A ripened mellowness which time alone
Bestows, a certain aristocracy
Of beam and sill. Old houses quietly
Observe a changing world, content to own
And cherish what old walls, old hearths,
  have known
Of tears and laughter, love and loyalty.

Old houses know the ways of human hearts...
The innocence of babes, the wild sweet pain
Of youth and love, the stillness of last sleep,
The touch of snow, the first pale bud that starts,
The ancient lullabies of wind and rain...
These thread the dreams old houses weave and keep.

Jessie Wilmore Murton

PRIVATE PLEASE
DO NOT ENTER

Readers' Reflections

A Place To Remember

Whenever we think of hometown
We see a town cozy and small
With spacious lawns blazing with flowers
And a welcoming smile for all.

But hometown could be a city
With its buildings brushing the sky
Or a cabin in the country
With the wilds of nature nearby.

For it is a part of childhood,
An Alice-in-Wonderland place,
Woven of dreams and remembrance
Which passing time cannot efface.

Catherine Grayman

Trains at Night

I like the whistle of trains at night,
The fast trains thundering by so proud!
They rush and rumble across the world,
They ring wild bells and they toot so loud!

But I love better the slower trains.
They take their time through the world instead,
And whistle softly and stop to tuck
Each sleepy blinking town in bed!

Frances Frost

Chimneys

I like the sight of chimney-tops
    Above a gabled town,
They have a smoky, friendly air
    As evening settles down.

They hint of opened oven doors,
    Of supper tables spread,
Of lamp-lit rooms and cheery talk
    And children safe in bed.

Leroy Alwin Wilton

Editor's Note: Readers are invited to submit poetry, short anecdotes, and humorous reflections on life for possible publication in future *Ideals* issues. *Ideals* pays $10 for each poem published and a negotiable fee for prose, depending on its quality and length.

My Hometown

The folks that live in my hometown
Are wonderful and true;
You'll never find more faithful friends
If you look the whole world through.

The spots I cherished as a child
Come back to me, and then,
For just a moment, I relive
Those happy days again.

The hills of home still beckon me,
And oft I do return
To visit scenes and folks I love —
Dear ones for whom I yearn.

There'll always be a cherished spot
Within my heart, 'tis true,
For my hometown and all the folks
Who've been so kind and true.

Eleanor Pederson Hillemann

Little Towns

I love the look of little towns
    Where one will always find
The neighbors up and down each street:
    The friendly, helpful kind.

I love the sweetness of small towns
    With fragrance in the air,
Where flowers bloom in every yard,
    With beauty everywhere.

I love the wealth of little towns
    Where the folks are able
To grow their gardens fresh and green
    For the family table.

I love the hope of little towns
    Where everyone, it seems,
Can work so well together there
    To realize fond dreams.

Virginia Katherine Oliver

But Not My Heart

These feet of mine might some day stray
To other countries, far away;
I might search pastures much more green
And find life's beauties in between.
Who knows the path that they might lead,
The times of joy, the times of need.
From fireside joys, I might depart;
My feet might stray — but not my heart.

Who knows the trials tomorrow holds,
The cares and burdens life unfolds;
For days won't always bring a smile
Nor each tomorrow be worthwhile.
Time changes many things, I know;
It changes dreams we treasure so.
And yet I've known it from the start;
The world moves on — but not my heart.

There are memories in this precious place,
To warm my soul and light my face;
The years have added wondrous love;
'Tis here I prayed to God above.
Whatever else, what-e'er might be,
This dear old place is part of me,
And though I roam, we'll never part;
My feet might stray — but not my heart.

Garnett Ann Schultz

To Your Little House

I shall remember candlelight
　And the low fire burning
When the only sound was a quiet word
　Or a book page turning.

I shall remember the song of the wind
　And the bias drive of rain
When cold days and dark days
　Beat at the windowpane.

Morning opened a golden fan
　In your elm tree,
And evening spread her colors out
　For your little house to see.

I must follow a dark road,
　A road that has no turning —
But I shall remember candlelight
　And the low fire burning.

Mildred Bowers Armstrong

Pastoral

Like homing birds my thoughts ever return
To quiet country lanes and cool, clear pools,
To mossy woods adorned with flowers and fern,
Uncomplicated by big city rules.
I want to follow the sound of waterfalls
Down craggy slopes to meadows far below,
To listen to the lilt of wild finch calls,
To rest where tranquil waters gently flow.
I want to flee from turmoil and from strife
When problems and worry grow intense,
Escape the clamor of the urban life
And follow my heart along an old rail fence,
Past laughing brooks and through sweet, new-cut hay,
To rest again at the close of day.

Elmera J. Cartwright

I gather thyme upon the sunny hills,
　　And its pure fragrance ever gladdens me,
　　And in my mind having tranquility
I smile to see how my green basket fills.
And by clear streams I gather daffodils;
　　And in dim woods find out the cherry tree,
　　And take its fruit and the wild strawberry
And nuts and honey; and live free from ills.
I dwell on the green earth, 'neath the blue sky,
　　Birds are my friends, and leaves my rustling roof:
The deer are not afraid of me, and I
　　Hear the wild goat, and hail its hastening hoof;
The squirrels sit perked as I pass them by,
　　And even the watchful hare stands not aloof.

Christina Rossetti

Haying

From the soft dike road, crooked and wagon-worn,
Comes the great load of rustling scented hay,
Slow-drawn with heavy swing and creaky sway
Through the cool freshness of the windless morn.
The oxen, yoked and sturdy, horn to horn,
Sharing the rest and toil of night and day,
Bend head and neck to the long hilly way
By many a season's labour marked and torn.
On the broad sea of dike the gathering heat
Waves upward from the grass, where road on road
Is swept before the tramping of the teams.
And while the oxen rest beside the sweet
New hay, the loft receives the early load,
With hissing stir, among the dusty beams.

John Frederic Herbin

The Hayloft

Through all the pleasant meadow-side
   The grass grew shoulder-high,
Till the shining scythes went far and wide
   And cut it down to dry.

These green and sweetly smelling crops
   They led in wagons home;
And they piled them here in mountain tops
   For mountaineers to roam.

Here is Mount Clear, Mount Rusty-Nail,
   Mount Eagle and Mount High;
The mice that in these mountains dwell,
   No happier are than I!

O what a joy to clamber there,
   O what a place for play,
With the sweet, the dim, the dusty air,
   The happy hills of hay!

Robert Louis Stevenson

Prairie Farmer

The Kranses were the nearest kinfolk we had in America except for the Holmes family in Galesburg. When John and Lena Krans bought their farm in the early 1870s, they worked from daylight to dark eight or nine months of the year till at last the mortgages were paid off. They had help from neighbors in getting in their crops and in turn helped the neighbors. The Kranses became part of the land they owned. Their feet wore paths that didn't change over the years — in the cow pasture with a small creek winding over it, the corn and oat fields, the vegetable garden, the potato patch. John Krans was a landsman, his thoughts never far from his land, the animals, the crops. He could talk about *hastarna,* meaning "horses," so to my mind he seemed part horse.

He was a medium-sized man but he had a loose easy way of carrying his shoulders with his head flung back so he gave the impression of being a big man. His eyes had gleam and his lips had a smile you could see through the beard. Even amid the four walls of a room his head, hair, and beard seemed to be in a high wind. When I sat on his knee and ran my five-year-old hand around in his beard, he called me *min lille gosse* ("my little boy") and there was a ripple of laughter and love in it. He read his Bible and sometimes a newspaper, though most often he liked to read the land and the sky, the ways of horses and corn. He wasn't an arguing man except that with a plow he could argue against stubborn land and with strong hands on leather reins he could argue with runaway horses.

Not often on Sunday did he miss hitching a horse to a light wagon and taking the family to the Lutheran church a mile or two away. I doubt whether he ever listened to a preacher who had less fear and more faith than he had. I have sometimes thought that John Krans pictured God as a Farmer whose chores were endless and inconceivable, that in this world and in worlds beyond God planted and tended and reaped His crops in mysterious ways past human understanding.

Carl Sandburg

From *Prairie-Town Boy,* copyright 1952, 1953 by Carl Sandburg; copyright renewed 1980, 1981 by Margaret Sandburg, Janet Sandburg, and Helga Sandburg Crile. Reprinted by permission of Harcourt Brace Jovanovich, Inc.

AMERICAN GOTHIC: Grant Wood; Collection of The Art Institute of Chicago.

Mowing

There was never a sound beside the wood but one,
And that was my long scythe whispering to the ground.
What was it it whispered? I knew not well myself;
Perhaps it was something about the heat of the sun,
Something, perhaps, about the lack of sound —
And that was why it whispered and did not speak.
It was no dream of the gift of idle hours,
Or easy gold at the hand of fay or elf:
Anything more than the truth would have seemed too weak
To the earnest love that laid the swale in rows,
Not without feeble-pointed spikes of flowers
(Pale orchises), and scared a bright green snake.
The fact is the sweetest dream that labor knows.
My long scythe whispered and left the hay to make.

Robert Frost

From *The Poetry of Robert Frost* edited by Edward Connery Lathem. Copyright 1934, © 1969 by Holt, Rinehart and Winston. Copyright © 1962 by Robert Frost. Reprinted by permission of Holt, Rinehart and Winston, Publishers.

The Sheaves

Where long the shadows of the wind had rolled,
Green wheat was yielding to the change assigned;
And as by some vast magic undivined
The world was turning slowly into gold.
Like nothing that was ever bought or sold
It waited there, the body and the mind;
And with a mighty meaning of a kind
That tells the more the more it is not told.

So in a land where all days are not fair,
Fair days went on till on another day
A thousand golden sheaves were lying there,
Shining and still, but not for long to stay —
As if a thousand girls with golden hair
Might rise from where they slept and go away.

Edwin Arlington Robinson

Reprinted with permission of Macmillan Company from *Collected Poems* by Edwin Arlington Robinson.
Copyright 1925 by Edwin Arlington Robinson, renewed 1953 by Ruth Nivison and Barbara R. Holt.

Overleaf
GRAIN ELEVATORS
Gene Ahrens

Some Quiet Stream

I would lie stretched out in a willow's shade
On the bank of a serpentine stream
Whose meanderings banished thoughts of haste,
I would watch the shiners' gleam
As they darted across the shiny bar
And the heat waves shimmered near and far;

I would have a book lying close at hand
To read as I pleased or not,
I would leave behind all my fishing gear,
For this is a kindly spot
Where I would not inflict the slightest pain,
But could bathe my soul when I come again.

I would watch the butterfly flutter by,
And the darning-needle poise,
And the water skippers with suction cups
Tread water without a noise;
I would glimpse the turtle out on his log
And in the lilies the waiting frog.

And the song of birds and the insects' hum
In the balmy summer breeze
Would banish quickly the world's humdrum,
And find me upon my knees
To thank the great God of everywhere
For His outdoor healing, in fervent prayer.

Luman Wesley Colton

Within the Bluegrass region the horse farms tend to be somewhat clustered and provide a distinctive landscape pattern. The scenic and aesthetic aspects are well known to tourists and treasured by urban dwellers in Lexington and surrounding towns. The farmscape is parklike with its grass covered rolling terrain and numerous majestic trees; plank fences extend along the roads and separate pastures; now and then an old stone fence remains by the roadside. The horse farm countryside affords a seasonal succession of landscape beauty. The soft green of spring, accented with the pink and white of dogwood, crab apples, and hawthorns, is the setting for the attentive mares with their tag-along, spindly legged foals. The rich verdure of summer gradually becomes the brilliant scarlet and gold of autumn, and the less colorful winterscape, to a greater extent than the more spectacular seasons, emphasizes the grace and beauty of the gentle undulations of the land.

The old stone fences, which may often be seen along roads bordering stock farms in the Bluegrass country, were laid without mortar, many of them a century and a half ago. A study by two geographers who were making a fence traverse for 825 miles between Cleveland, Ohio, and Athens, Georgia, revealed that stone fences were restricted to stock-raising areas with available rock and were found to any considerable extent only in the Inner Bluegrass of Kentucky. Thus they are unique, historic, and part of the local culture. Bonding without mortar requires more skill, experience, time, and patience than a mortared wall re-quires, and today it is almost a lost art.

Horse barns are architecturally interesting and surprisingly luxurious. They are well constructed and beautifully maintained, with interiors of fine wood accented with polished brass accessories. Most of them are covered with clapboard painted according to a color scheme followed uniformly throughout a farm, as are employees' residences and other farm buildings. Sometimes a farm's colors are those of its racing silks. Most of the frame barns have cupolas and dormer windows; if there is an entrance on the long side, it is surmounted by a pediment or gable frequently bearing a Palladian window. Some of the old barns were built of stone, some of brick, and some of stone and brick combined. A few special ones have clock towers. Most of the recent ones are constructed of fireproof concrete block and painted according to the farm's color scheme.

If one calls to mind a typical "mansion house" (to use an old term) on a horse farm, it would be a stately Greek Revival structure with tall white columns, standing in formal dignity atop a gentle hill. It is true that there are many of these, and so appropriate is the style that when a large and well constructed residence on a Bluegrass estate happens to have been built in an eclectic style during the late Victorian period, it is likely to be thoroughly remodeled and given a colossal order portico. However, if one surveys the residences on Bluegrass horse farms, one finds represented every period in the history of Kentucky architecture.

Photo opposite
MARE AND FOAL
Grant Heilman

Reprinted from *The Horse World of the Bluegrass*, copyright 1980, by Jim Host and Associates, Inc., 120 Kentucky Avenue, Lexington, Kentucky 40502.

Ode to the South

Gently rolling lands
plantations, farms — ranches
dotted by the houses of memories
majestic in stance
of a flowering past —
elegant brick walks
tall red brick chimney — burning
green grass —
lined with shrubs and bushes,
magnolia blossoms, pecan trees
soybean fields — rice
catfish ponds
and cotton patch.

William Lowenkamp

Virginia's Calling Me

I love the sunny Southland
  where the orange blossoms grow;
And a thousand miles remove you
  from chilling ice and snow;
I love her lakes and rivers
  and the beauties of her seas;
Her soft enchanting moonlight,
  and her cool refreshing breeze.
But with all her heavenly glory,
  my old heart longs to go
To my home in Old Virginia
  and friends of long ago.

Take me back along the pathways
  my naked feet have trod,
Where the beauties of nature
  bring me nearer still to God,
Let me roam the fields and meadows
  and stately wooded hills
And hear the silvery music
  of the waterfalls and rills
And drink the golden glory
  of the sunset's afterglow
'Round my home in Old Virginia,
  with friends of long ago.

Edwin C. Davis

Take Me Back to My Old Home Town

Let me fish again,
Under the wagon bridge,
On the banks of the old bayou,
Where as a barefoot boy,
I would lie and dream,
When my morning chores were through.

Let me climb once more,
To the crest of the bluff,
And gaze beneath sun-kissed skies,
At the world below,
Where I would see afar,
A panorama of Paradise.

So take me again,
On a cold wintry day,
To the hill where I once slid down.
O let me have once more,
All the joy of my youth,
And the beauty of my home town.

A. Phil Londroche

Painting opposite
FRIENDS
John Campbell

Often I think of the beautiful town
That is seated by the sea;
Often in thought go up and down
The pleasant streets of that dear old town,
And my youth comes back to me.
And a verse of a Lapland song
Is haunting my memory still:
  "A boy's will is the wind's will,
And the thoughts of youth are long, long thoughts."

I can see the shadowy lines of its trees,
And catch, in sudden gleams,
The sheen of the far-surrounding seas,
And islands that were the Hesperides
Of all my boyish dreams.
And the burden of that old song,
It murmurs and whispers still:
  "A boy's will is the wind's will,
And the thoughts of youth are long, long thoughts."

I remember the black wharves and the slips,
And the sea-tides tossing free;
And Spanish sailors with bearded lips,
And the beauty and mystery of the ships,
And the magic of the sea.
And the voice of that wayward song
Is singing and saying still:
  "A boy's will is the wind's will,
And the thoughts of youth are long, long thoughts."

I remember the bulwarks by the shore,
And the fort upon the hill;
The sunrise gun, with its hollow roar,
The drum-beat repeated o'er and o'er,
And the bugle wild and shrill.
And the music of that old song
Throbs in my memory still:
  "A boy's will is the wind's will,
And the thoughts of youth are long, long thoughts."

I remember the sea-fight far away,
How it thundered o'er the tide!
And the dead captains, as they lay
In their graves, o'erlooking the tranquil bay,
Where they in battle died.
And the sound of that mournful song
Goes through me with a thrill:
  "A boy's will is the wind's will,
And the thoughts of youth are long, long thoughts."

My Lost

Youth

I can see the breezy dome of groves,
The shadows of Deering's Woods;
And the friendships old and the early loves
Come back with a Sabbath sound, as of doves
In quiet neighborhoods.
And the verse of that sweet old song,
It flutters and murmurs still:
   "A boy's will is the wind's will,
And the thoughts of youth are long, long thoughts."

I remember the gleams and glooms that dart
Across the school-boy's brain;
The song and the silence in the heart,
That in part are prophecies, and in part
Are longings wild and vain.
And the voice of that fitful song
Sings on, and is never still:
   "A boy's will is the wind's will,
And the thoughts of youth are long, long thoughts."

There are things of which I may not speak;
There are dreams that cannot die;
There are thoughts that make the strong heart weak,
And bring a pallor into the cheek,
And a mist before the eye.
And the words of that fatal song
Come over me like a chill:
   "A boy's will is the wind's will,
And the thoughts of youth are long, long thoughts."

Strange to me now are the forms I meet
When I visit the dear old town;
But the native air is pure and sweet,
And the trees that o'ershadow each well-known street,
As they balance up and down,
Are singing the beautiful song,
Are sighing and whispering still:
   "A boy's will is the wind's will,
And the thoughts of youth are long, long thoughts."

And Deering's Woods are fresh and fair,
And with joy that is almost pain
My heart goes back to wander there,
And among the dreams of the days that were,
I find my lost youth again.
And the strange and beautiful song,
The groves are repeating it still:
   "A boy's will is the wind's will,
And the thoughts of youth are long, long thoughts."

Henry Wadsworth Longfellow

Life on the Mississippi

The face of the water, in time, became a wonderful book — a book that was a dead language to the uneducated passenger, but which told its mind to me without reserve, delivering its most cherished secrets as clearly as if it uttered them with a voice. And it was not a book to be read once and thrown aside, for it had a new story to tell every day. Throughout the long twelve hundred miles there was never a page that was void of interest, never one that you could leave unread without loss, never one that you would want to skip, thinking you could find higher enjoyment in some other thing. There never was so wonderful a book written by man; never one whose interest was so absorbing, so unflagging, so sparklingly renewed with every reperusal. The passenger who could not read it was charmed with a peculiar sort of faint dimple on its surface (on the rare occasions when he did not overlook it altogether); but to the pilot that was an *italicized* passage; indeed, it was more than that, it was a legend of the largest capitals, with a string of shouting

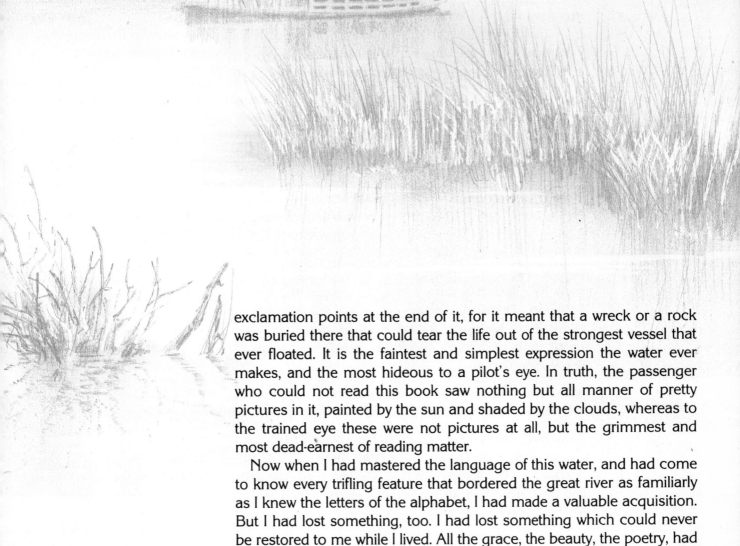

exclamation points at the end of it, for it meant that a wreck or a rock was buried there that could tear the life out of the strongest vessel that ever floated. It is the faintest and simplest expression the water ever makes, and the most hideous to a pilot's eye. In truth, the passenger who could not read this book saw nothing but all manner of pretty pictures in it, painted by the sun and shaded by the clouds, whereas to the trained eye these were not pictures at all, but the grimmest and most dead-earnest of reading matter.

Now when I had mastered the language of this water, and had come to know every trifling feature that bordered the great river as familiarly as I knew the letters of the alphabet, I had made a valuable acquisition. But I had lost something, too. I had lost something which could never be restored to me while I lived. All the grace, the beauty, the poetry, had gone out of the majestic river!

Mark Twain

Gateway to the West

Man is capable of a limitless vision. The ability of our minds to imagine, together with the ability of our hands to build, allows man to dream his future and build that future according to his imaginings.

A city like St. Louis can be thought of as a kind of culmination of the visions and dreams of many men. A city grows, as St. Louis did, from such meager dreams as the building of a log cabin on the west banks of the Mississippi River in 1764, where Pierre Laclede and Auguste Chouteau opened their fur-trading post.

On the banks of the Mississippi River at St. Louis, surrounded by a twentieth-century metropolis, we can look back at what came before us down the long river of geologic time, and we can look off toward the future and wonder which of man's imaginings will become reality in the year 2000 and beyond.

If future man comes upon this stainless-steel arch, the result of one man's imaginings, he will have some notion of our dreams for the future. Stand under the Gateway Arch some full-moon night and listen as it reaches toward the stars and returns with their light. The arch is also a tribute to the dreams of our past: to the dreams of men like Thomas Jefferson, who negotiated the purchase of the Louisiana Territory; to the dreams of the explorers with Lewis and Clark, who headed west up the Missouri River in May 1804. After more than two years and 7,000 miles, they brought back word of the Pacific Ocean.

Measure the speed of jets across America today against the years since 1804. Man's imagination propels him quickly into the future.

Man has always been an explorer adventuring out beyond the circle of fire, out beyond the flat maps of ancient cartographers marked with warnings that read "Here Be Monsters," out beyond the pull of earth's gravity. Man's future has first been man's dream of that future.

Reprinted from *Missouri: Faces and Places*, by Wes Lyle and John Hall, copyright © 1977, by The Regents Press of Kansas (now University Press of Kansas).

The Town I Knew

The town I knew when I was small
Had nestled close beside the shore.
It wasn't very big at all —
A single street of stores and shops,
Some churches, schools, and growing crops,
Smoke curling from home chimney tops;
Such was the town I knew.

The town I knew was never rushed,
Sunrise was beautiful and bright,
Sunset was glorious and hushed.
The people were a friendly sort
Not given to unkind retort
Nor swayed by slanderous report;
Such was the town I knew.

The town I knew had two long piers
Where steamboats came across the bay,
And I can see yet through the years
A shore train pull around the bend,
Stop here and there, and slowly wend
Its way to that pier journey's end;
Such was the town I knew.

The town I knew was quiet, too,
After the steamboat steamed away;
So still that I hear yet today
The rattle of a loosened plank,
A seaman's call, a chain's rude clank,
A boat's swish as it rose and sank;
Such was the town I knew.

The town I knew, today is gone;
In fifty years the tide has turned.
Self-service travel has returned,
Small pleasure craft now line the shore,
Steamboats and railroad are no more,
But in my dreams, just as before
The town I knew lives on.

C. A. Lufburrow

JAY KILLIAN

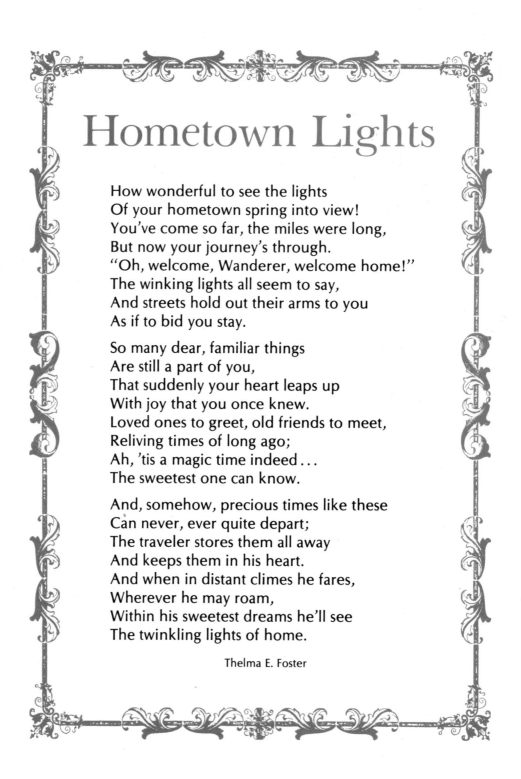

Hometown Lights

How wonderful to see the lights
Of your hometown spring into view!
You've come so far, the miles were long,
But now your journey's through.
"Oh, welcome, Wanderer, welcome home!"
The winking lights all seem to say,
And streets hold out their arms to you
As if to bid you stay.

So many dear, familiar things
Are still a part of you,
That suddenly your heart leaps up
With joy that you once knew.
Loved ones to greet, old friends to meet,
Reliving times of long ago;
Ah, 'tis a magic time indeed...
The sweetest one can know.

And, somehow, precious times like these
Can never, ever quite depart;
The traveler stores them all away
And keeps them in his heart.
And when in distant climes he fares,
Wherever he may roam,
Within his sweetest dreams he'll see
The twinkling lights of home.

Thelma E. Foster

Photo opposite
VICTORIA, BRITISH COLUMBIA
Gene Ahrens

Edna Jaques

Edna Jaques, one of Canada's most noted poets, was born in Collingwood, Ontario, on January 17, 1891. Her parents were rural people who taught their children to cherish the land and domestic life. From this arose an appreciation of simple pleasures like aromatic kitchens, glowing fireplaces, and crisp breezes. These are celebrated in Mrs. Jaques's poetry.

At age seven Edna Jaques wrote her first poems. She hid them in nooks and corners, reading them only to herself. When she was sixteen, the young poet left school to give more time to writing. She soon submitted a packet of poems to *The Herald Times* in Saskatchewan. They were accepted and published. That newspaper would be the first publisher of her books. *The Vancouver Sun Province* also recognized Mrs. Jaques's potential as a poet and agreed to publish ten of her poems every month. This arrangement continued for twenty years. In 1975 the people of Ontario honored Edna Jaques by naming her "outstanding woman of the Province for International Women's Year."

Collingwood, Ontario

It was a little town that cradled me,
Behind it rose blue hills to meet the sky,
And by its threshold lapped an inland sea
Where little puffy boats went sailing by.

And I remember cool unhurried lanes
Where bare brown feet went pattering up and down,
With old back yards and orchards in the sun
Behind the stately houses of the town.

Gay playmates of a happy childhood land,
Fences to walk and swaying trees to climb,
Old broken dishes set against a wall,
And all the glowing kingdom that was mine.

New bread with flaky crusts and lots of jam,
Cookies with scalloped edges crisp and thin,
Gardens to dig for treasures in the sand,
Small creeks to wade and fish for minnows in.

Old ladies primly sitting on the lawn,
Green tangled hedges growing wild and dense,
Old fashioned flowers nodding in the sun:
We peeked at them through knot-holes in the fence.

Ah, dear enchanted land that gave us birth,
Gave us her soil, her hidden ways to know,
Pathways to bear the imprint of our feet,
Making us hers, wherever we might go.

The Home Paper

Four little sheets, their printing smudged and blurred
   And yet the old folks read it word for word,
They're living at the Coast...and all they know
   Is back there in a land of wind and snow.
That's why they left, they couldn't stand the cold,
   For blood runs thin and sluggish when you're old.

And now they sit among their blooming flowers
   In solid comfort...yet the summer hours
Drag by and there is nothing much to do,
   No baking...when you only cook for two,
You buy the bread...and dad just never took
   To passing long, long hours with a book.

They love their little garden and the way
   The lawn stays green...and in the month of May
The trees flame out like brides to greet the spring,
   And all the holy bells of Heaven ring
Across the lawn where daisies nod their heads
   And hold communion in their sunny beds.

Yet when the little old home paper comes
   They gloat above it, all the tiny crumbs
Of news, they gather up like miser's gold;
   Pour over all the paragraphs and hold
The sheets aside and talk with eyes aglow
   Of dear old neighbors of the long ago.

For every item is a personal thing,
   They know the folks, and so the columns ring
Small bells within their hearts, for they can see
   The faces of old neighbors tenderly,
And though they go their lonely ways apart
   Still they are members of a small town's heart.

A Sea-Port Town

Always a whisper of the sea,
   A wind that tugs at the heart of me,
Deep throated whistles across the bay,
   Old fishermen smoking on the quay,
Telling a yarn with a whispered end,
   And a ready hand to an old time friend.

An old tramp steamer with crusted sides,
   The seethe and pull of the changing tides,
A salty taste to the flying spray,
   Sea-gulls crying at dawn of day,
Always the hunger gnawing there,
   For the wind and the road to God-knows-where.

For a little garden may hold me close,
   A bordered walk and the look of a rose,
But under it all like a hunted thing,
   The fog and the wind's whispering.
For my heart will follow what e'er befall,
   The sound of the waves and the wind's call.

Little Towns

Little towns are lovely places,
   Cool wide streets and friendly faces,
Neighbors running in and out,
   Women middle-aged and stout,
Grandmas with old silver hair,
   Like a halo shining there.

In a little town there seems
   Time for happiness and dreams,
Time to visit folks — to grow
   Into ways that people know.
Life all bound with tender strands
   Woven by their friendly hands.

I like little towns, for here
   People grow so close and dear,
Funerals, weddings, death and birth,
   All the good and bad of earth,
Cloudy skies and days that shine
   Shared like sacramental wine.

Overleaf
ORLEANS, CAPE COD
Fred Dole

Voice of America

I am the cornfields of the Middle West,
Rustling and whispering in the prairie breeze,
The snow-capped Rockies pointing to the sky.
I am youth's ambitions, symbols of these:

The cotton fields and bluegrass of the South
That stand for gracious hospitality,
The spirit of undefeated statehood
And antebellum aristocracy.

I am the rolling voice of crested waves
Inviting all within my Golden Gate,
The vast Pacific of the vibrant West,
With shore and climate sure to captivate.

I am America! Its eastern towns,
Its rocky hillsides and its winding streams,
The sacrifices of the Founding Fathers,
The torch that lit the pathway to their dreams.

I am the cities: Chicago, and New York,
All magic towns part of our wondrous nation,
I am the flag that proudly waves aloft
For freedom and for its commemoration.

Stella Craft Tremble

I Hear America Singing

I hear America singing, the varied carols I hear,
Those of mechanics, each one singing his as it should be blithe and strong,
The carpenter singing his as he measures his plank or beam,
The mason singing his as he makes ready for work, or leaves off work,
The boatman singing what belongs to him in his boat, the deckhand singing on the steamboat deck,
The shoemaker singing as he sits on his bench, the hatter singing as he stands,
The wood-cutter's song, the ploughboy's on his way in the morning, or at noon intermission or
   at sundown,
The delicious singing of the mother, or of the young wife at work, or of the girl sewing or washing,
Each singing what belongs to him or her and to none else,
The day what belongs to the day — at night the party of young fellows, robust, friendly,
Singing with open mouths their strong melodious songs.

Walt Whitman

Overleaf
GOLDEN GATE BRIDGE
Bob Clemenz

America for Me

It's fine to see the Old World, and travel up and down
Among the famous palaces and cities of renown,
To admire the crumbly castles and the statues of the kings —
But now I think I've had enough of antiquated things.

So it's home again, and home again, America for me!
My heart is turning home again, and there I long to be,
In the land of youth and freedom beyond the ocean bars,
Where the air is full of sunlight and the flag is full of stars.

Oh, London is a man's town, there's power in the air;
And Paris is a woman's town, with flowers in her hair;
And it's sweet to dream in Venice, and it's great to study Rome;
But when it comes to living there is no place like home.

I like the German fir-woods, in green battalions drilled;
I like the gardens of Versailles with flashing fountains filled;
But, oh, to take your hand, my dear, and ramble for a day
In the friendly western woodland where Nature has her way!

I know that Europe's wonderful, yet something seems to lack:
The Past is too much with her, and the people looking back.
But the glory of the Present is to make the Future free —
We love our land for what she is and what she is to be.

Oh, it's home again, and home again, America for me!
I want a ship that's westward bound to plough the rolling sea,
To the blessed Land of Room Enough beyond the ocean bars,
Where the air is full of sunlight and the flag is full of stars.

Henry van Dyke

Pictures of growing spring and farms and homes,
With the Fourth-month eve at sundown, and the gray smoke lucid and
    bright,
With floods of the yellow gold of the gorgeous, indolent, sinking sun,
    burning, expanding the air,
With the fresh sweet herbage under foot, and the pale green leaves of
    the trees prolific,
In the distance the flowing glaze, the breast of the river, with a wind-
    dapple here and there,
With ranging hills on the banks, with many a line against the sky, and
    shadows,
And the city at hand with dwellings so dense, and stacks of chimneys,
And all the scenes of life and the workshops, and the workmen home-
    ward returning.

Lo, body and soul — this land,
My own Manhattan with spires, and the sparkling and hurrying tides,
    and the ships,
The varied and ample land, the South and the North in the light, Ohio's
    shores and flashing Missouri,
And ever the far-spreading prairies cover'd with grass and corn.

Lo, the most excellent sun so calm and haughty,
The violet and purple morn with just-felt breezes,
The gentle soft-born measureless light,
The miracle spreading bathing all, the fulfill'd noon,
The coming eve delicious, the welcome night and the stars,
Over my cities shining all, enveloping man and land.

                              Walt Whitman

The Homecoming

by Thomas Wolfe

All through the night George lay in his dark berth and watched the old earth of Virginia as it stroked past him in the dream-haunted silence of the moon. Field and hill and gulch and stream and wood again, the everlasting earth, the huge illimitable earth of America, kept stroking past him in the steep silence of the moon.

All through the ghostly stillness of the land, the train made on forever its tremendous noise, fused of a thousand sounds, and they called back to him forgotten memories: old songs, old faces, old memories, and all strange, wordless, and unspoken things men know and live and feel, and never find a language for — the legend of dark time, the sad brevity of their days, the unknowable but haunting miracle of life itself. He heard again, as he had heard throughout his childhood, the pounding wheel, the tolling bell, the whistle-wail, and he remembered how these sounds, coming to him from the river's edge

in the little town of his boyhood, had always evoked for him their tongueless prophecy of wild and secret joy, their glorious promises of new lands, mornings, and a shining city. But now the lonely cry of the great train was speaking to him with an equal strangeness of return. For he was going home again.

The undertone of terror with which he had gone to bed, the sadness of the fore-shadowed changes in the town, the somber prospect of the funeral tomorrow, all combined to make him dread his home-coming, which so many times in the years since he had been away he had looked forward to some day with hope and exultation. It was all so different from what he thought it would be. He was still only an obscure instructor at one of the universities in the city, his book was not yet published, he was not by any standard which his native town could know — "successful," "a success." And as he thought of it, he realized that, almost more than any-

ACKNOWLEDGEMENTS

TO YOUR LITTLE HOUSE from TWIST O' SMOKE by Mildred Bowers Armstrong. Published by Yale University Press. TRAINS AT NIGHT by Frances Frost. From BRIDLED WITH RAINBOWS © Copyright 1949, Macmillan Co., New York, New York. THE HOME TOWN by Edgar A. Guest. Reprinted with permission. Recipes for HOMEMADE ICE CREAM by Darlene Kronschnabel. HARMONY HERITAGE by James McClelland, reprinted from a pamphlet, courtesy of the Society for the Preservation and Encouragement of Barber Shop Quartet Singing in America, Inc. OLD HOUSES from GRACE NOTES by Jessie Wilmore Murton. Copyright 1960 by Review and Herald Publishing Association. BUT NOT MY HEART from BUT NOT MY HEART by Garnett Ann Schultz, copyright 1969. Published by Dorrance & Company. I REMEMBER A TOWN from DOWN THIS ROAD REMEMBERING by Sheila Stinson, copyright 1949. AMERICA FOR ME from COLLECTED POEMS by Henry van Dyke. Our sincere thanks to the following authors whose addresses we were unable to locate: Luman Wesley Colton for SOME QUIET STREAM; Dana Craig for THOSE OLD MODEL T'S; Edwin C. Davis for VIRGINIA'S CALLING ME; John F. Herbin for HAYING, from CANADIAN POETRY IN ENGLISH, Copyright 1954 by Ryerson Press, Toronto; A. Phil Londroche for TAKE ME BACK TO MY OLD HOME TOWN from I AM MISSISSIPPI by A. Phil Londroche, copyright 1954; Phyllis I. Rosenteur for THE CANDY STORE; and Leroy Alwin Wilton for CHIMNEYS.

thing, he feared the sharp, appraising eye, the worldly judgments, of that little town.

He thought of all his years away from home, the years of wandering in many lands and cities. He remembered how many times he had thought of home with such an intensity of passion that he could close his eyes and see the scheme of every street, and every house upon each street, and the faces of the people, as well as recall the countless things that they had said and the densely-woven fabric of all their histories. Tomorrow he would see it all again, and he almost wished he had not come. It would have been easy to plead the excuse of work and other duty. And it was silly, anyhow, to feel as he did about the place.

But why had he always felt so strongly the magnetic pull of home, why had he thought so much about it and remembered it with such blazing accuracy, if it did not matter, and if this little town, and the immortal hills

around it, was not the only home he had on earth? He did not know. All that he knew was that the years flow by like water, and that one day men come home again.

The train rushed onward through the moonlit land.

From YOU CAN'T GO HOME AGAIN by Thomas Wolfe, Copyright 1934, 1937, 1938, 1939, 1940 by Maxwell Perkins as Executor. Copyright renewed 1968 by Paul Gitlin, Administrator, C.T.A.

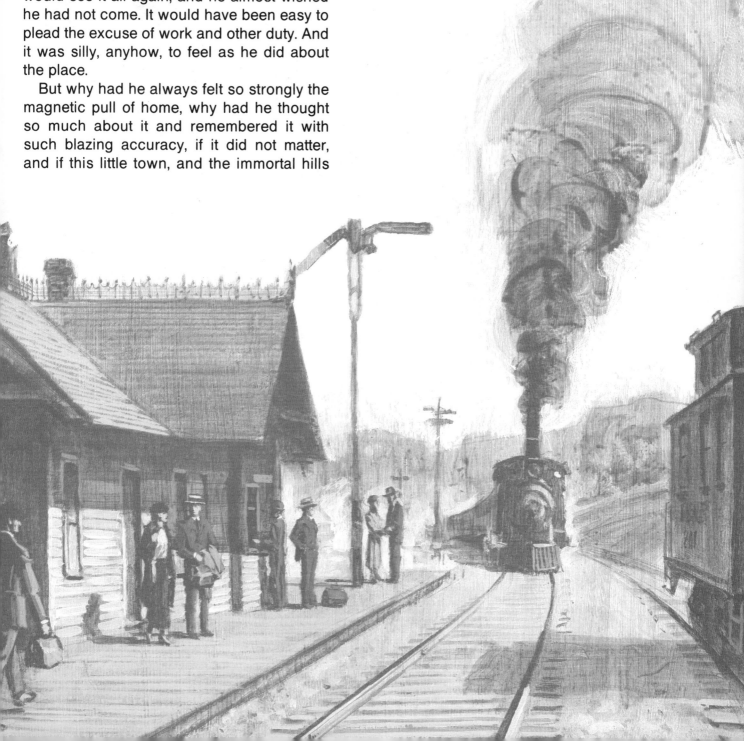

It's Our
40th Birthday!
IDEALS 1944-1984

Join us in a celebration of nature's most amiable season in our next anniversary issue, Summertime Ideals.

Enjoy the magic of midsummer nights, the romance of hot air ballooning, the thrill of sailing, the taste of homegrown watermelons.

Butterflies, sunsets, beaches, gorgeous flowers, colorful scenics ... our spectacular color photography helps you welcome the warmth of summer.

Complete with classic poetry and nostalgic prose, Summertime Ideals is the perfect gift for family and friends. Share the beauty of Ideals year round with a gift subscription today.